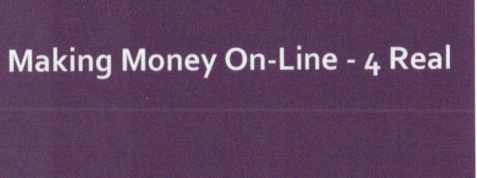

Making Money On-Line - 4 Real

A business plan for on-line money making, that works!

Let me give you the tools to succeed on-line with little to no investment or upfront cost!

Unemployed? Laid off? Just need extra income? Want your own business?

I have a proven plan for you, just read my plans and you will know right away that this will work and is very easy to get started using free advertising, like Facebook and other social media applications!

I will give you the ideas & steps to get the money & jobs flowing, no worries, this is a proven method of making money on-line that does in fact work very well!

Don't miss this opportunity, you will thank me later!

The Business Plan

A no bullshit approach to finding a job & making Money on-line the easy, no scams way! All you need is internet access, a small amount of social media knowledge, transportation of some type!

The Business

The Pickup & Delivery People! You can create your own business name!

Simple But Profitable

Everyday families purchase groceries, carry-out from restaurants, pickup & deliver packages from stores & other businesses. These tasks are time consuming and down-right dull to many of you. Wouldn't it be awesome if there were people to take some or all of these tasks over for us, for a small fee? Think about it, you need to get some groceries out in the county to an elderly family member but, you are strapped for time & have many things you need to do at your own home after work. What about just simple carry-out delivery, people love delivery & carry-out yet most restaurants or fast food joints do not offer carry-out delivery, but a cool team of worker bees could take over or handle many of these tasks for you and make some cash for their trouble! Great Idea Right? Why not be the person who does the pickup and delivery for a small fee? Why not be the company people call on to get those deliveries taken care of? This is where you can just be a worker bee and handle the task for a fee or you could become a business owner, farm out these tasks to a hand-picked team of worker bees!

The Sky is the limit

You could be making bucks all day long, helping other people with tasks that they either are tired of doing or just simply don't have the time. Think about all the people who have no transportation or need assistance for other reasons. What about businesses who need parts to complete their work, they could use a hand too. Think about, picking up items for people out of town while they work, what would that be worth? So many tasks that you could offer to handle for people & businesses in your community or surrounding area.

Do you see how easy this can be?

Service type work is always needed, so you never run out of tasks to make money with. You can do the tasks or why not start your own business with a team of worker bees completing task that you manage for the team?

Get your team together before putting your business into live mode, be ready for multiple tasks, locations, types of tasks!

So simple even a child could do this on a bicycle!

I hope you can now see how easy this can be to make money on-line! You can add your own ideas for service & make your new job or business even more profitable!

Carry-Outs can be a huge profit maker, not only will you make money, you will be promoting business for other businesses in your area! So you can see how this is a win-win situation for all!

Let your local businesses know that you will be providing a service, at no cost to them! They will love you for it and most likely this will build trust and loyalty with them!

Yay! Delivery for all!!!!

Your community will love that and love you for what you do for them!

The businesses will love you too, saves & makes them money at the same time with less overhead or drama of trying to hire and keep a staff for delivery!

Become the glue that holds the town together & the

important piece of the community puzzle!

The business owners will be dancing in the streets! Elated that they all have delivery help & options, they will most likely be loyal to you and spread the word about your services!

You can build a professional courteous team of task runners, manage your staff while they bring in the profits, giving you a residual income, yes make money while you sleep, the gift that keeps on giving!

Are you already starting to think of more ideas to make your new business huge?

I'm sure you are!

Use my plan along with your own ideas to make for one beautiful future for you and your family!

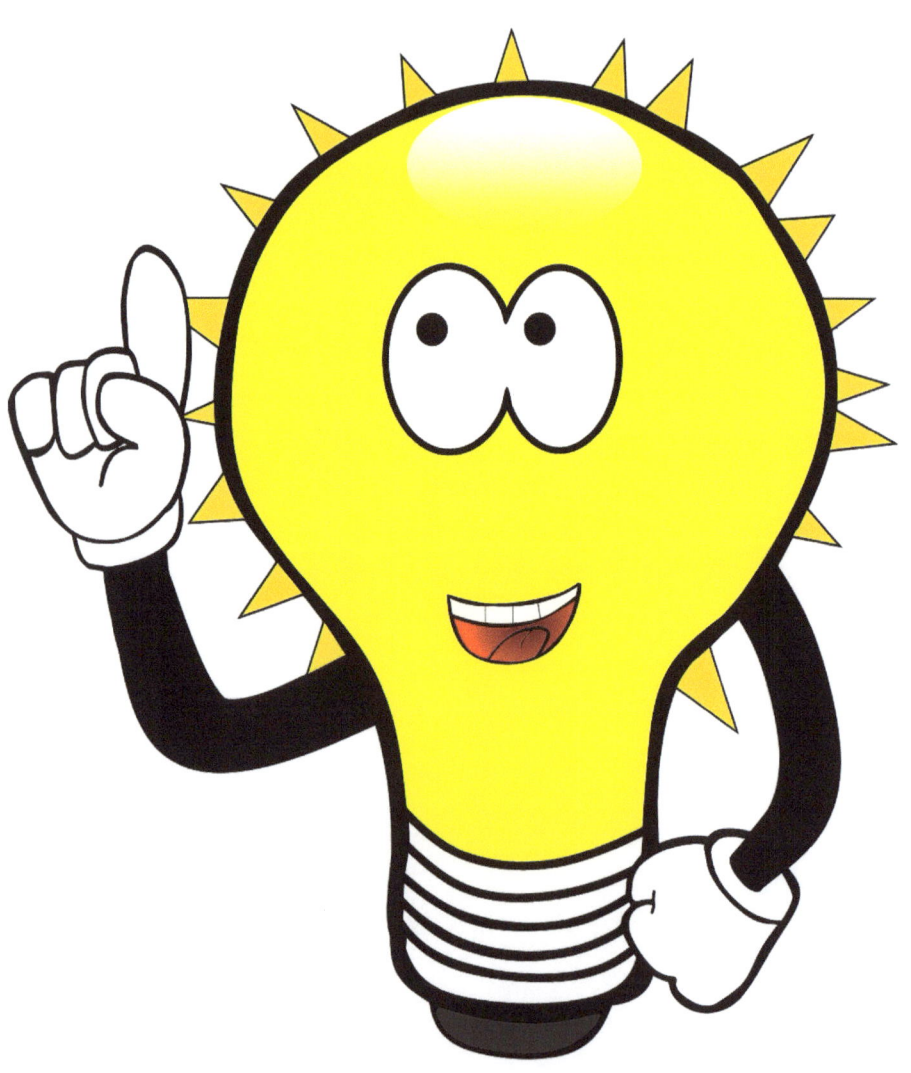

It's your birthday! It's your birthday! Birth of new job, birth of new business, birth of great ideas, heck it may even be your birthdate, so order a cake, have it delivered by a team member! Share the wealth!

You would promote your own business and team right? Sure you would!

Careful! Make sure your customers are legal age for some pickup & deliveries! Check state & local laws!

Ok, hold it, you need to have a license for some deliveries!!! Let's leave those for the trained professionals except in emergencies!

Again, this also might be a time when you can be of great help! Let the customers know if you provide special services!

Storage or delivery options, pickup packages options and more!

Social media groups, social media friends are free advertisement audiences, so make the most of getting the word out about your business or services offered totally free!

Facebook

Twitter

Instagram

Google Hangouts

Google Friends

Email lists

Bulletin Boards on-line & out in some stores

Flyers

Newspaper

Phone books

Magazines

Vinyl graphics on your vehicles

Signs

Send up smoke signals too (anything to promote your brand) Just kidding about smoke signals!

Radio & TV (how big do you want to grow your business)

Mail

Airplane Banners? Do you live near the beach or large public places, may not be a bad idea!

For your Team

Find help from friends & family, use contract labor to compensate, PayPal or other internet quick pay options, yes get paid before you provide services if you desire!

Setup a Facebook group for your services

Setup an email account specifically for your team

Setup a chat group with text messaging on your phone or other apps like Google Hangouts, Facebook Groups, or others

Advertise on all social media groups and everywhere you can that is free, then advertise in your local paper & phonebook if you want to grow your business!

Thanks for reading my tips & plans for creating cash flow, businesses & residual income. I hope you enjoy them & most of all I hope you are in the process of making real income with my ideas, real soon!

If you follow my plan and add ideas of your own, I see big things in your future!

Let's be that delivery person that everyone needs and make that fast cash!

So many ways to provide services and make a profit for your work!

You can add your own ideas to make this business as big as you would like!

Kenneth S. Davis

Business Ideas & Solutions

All rights reserved!© Other business names mentioned above are for informational purposes only and are not affiliated with myself or my company. All material suggested is merely just that, a suggestion to grow your pay & business!

Get going, this will work, it will help you make a good living and take out the middle man! BE YOUR OWN BOSS!

www.ingramcontent.com/pod-product-compliance
Lightning Source LLC
Chambersburg PA
CBHW041121180526
45172CB00001B/358